# The Witch on Yellowhammer Hill

## &
## Other poems

## Carla Martin-Wood

**Front cover** "The Witch on Yellowhammer Hill" montage ©2016, Carla Martin-Wood; rose photos ©2016, Carla Martin-Wood; owl, book and bunny photos public domain sourced from pixabay.com per Creative Commons CC0 https://creativecommons.org/publicdomain/zero/1.0/deed.en; all remaining bird, butterfly and moon photos ©2016, Brenda Levy Tate

**Back cover art** © Ateliersommerland, licensed via Dreamstime.com, ID 30379160

See complete list of photography and art credits listed under Acknowledgements in the final pages of this book.

**The 99% Press**
**poetry for the people**
**2016**

*The 99% Press thanks Brenda Levy Tate for her kind generosity in sharing her photography in this book.*

*This book is for Gaia.*

# About this book

*The Witch on Yellowhammer Hill* provides an enchanting glimpse into the unexpected magick of the poet's retirement and aging. What a surprise to find age celebrated! What joy to live each day with the freedom to read bedtime stories to flowers, to splash in rain puddles or chase fireflies on her cane, not giving a fig what neighbors may think!

Within these pages, we meet the Cailleach, an ancient Celtic hag Goddess who transforms into a beautiful young woman. We dance to the tribal energy of *womanpoem* and listen to the wisdom of *Crone's Counsel*. This is a poet who converses with a shrew, a grasshopper, and all disillusioned Cinderellas.

Yet amidst the joy and celebration, Martin-Wood also deftly steps from the world of fantasy to address the brutal realities of child abuse, bullying, our endangered environment, and the Charlie Hebdo massacre in Paris.

This is the poet's most comprehensive collection to date. In addition to over 50 new poems, readers will find selections from her previously published works, including several of her sonnets, her environmental poems, her most requested poems from two decades of public readings, and an entire section of her beloved nature poems.

The 99% Press
Poetry for the People

# Poems

**Poems from *Season of Mists* & more**

**About the poet**

**Acknowledgements**

# The Witch on Yellowhammer Hill

# The Witch on Yellowhammer Hill

I am the old lady who lives
across the street
I am the one who hobbles about on a cane
amongst butterflies in the morning
who talks to them
in a tongue unknown to you
who giggles when they dip down
to flutter-kiss my face
I am the one you watch cautiously
who stumbles in amongst your children
as they chase fireflies at twilight
who squeals just like they do
when one lights upon a finger.

I am the one you whisper about
who sings to the mockingbird
the one who makes you gasp
when he copies my tune
I am the one you heard
howl at the full moon
who leaves silver coins
in a circle beneath the oak tree
the one who bakes questionable brownies
whose shoulder once provided
a perch for the chickadee
I am the one the hummer dive bombs
to say good morning.

I am the old lady
who rocks Mitty-minded on my porch
graciously accepting Pulitzers
for masterpieces you will never read
who ambles out in an evening gown
to tell the flowers a story

and you swear that you saw them
bend toward me once to listen
the one who left you speechless
when you saw me stagger
about the grocer's parking lot
in a downpour
making puddlelicious splashes
and laughter.

Oh, I am the one they warned you about
when you first moved in
the moss-brained old lady
who has forgotten all the rules
of marketplace manlogic
how to work and worry
what is appropriate
who lost my to-do lists
my calendar
and a few marbles along the way
the one who dares not care
what you think
who prefers the company
of ladybugs and fairies
who doesn't answer
phone or doorbell anymore.

I am the old lady across the street
who woke up one day
and suddenly remembered
everything that matters.

# Spring at St. Martins

What is this green
and this fathomless glory
fresh from earth's belly
this gift so divine
born of life's lust
for itself everlasting
crocus by snowdrop
butterfly, dragonfly
tulip by pansy
hummingbird, wren
jonquil by daisy
bumble by firefly
from the four corners
spring rises again
no trumpets needed
no fanfare required
she covers the scars
of winter's despair
no trace is left
of its death and its sorrow
she pardons everything
offers tomorrow
time and again.

There in the hospice
high in the window
a woman is counting
her moments away
hour by minute
by breath and by heartbeat
she counts every petal
she counts every wing.

# Visitation at Samhain

Veil thins to nothing
spirits and shades glide gossamer
ride the chill October air
they console not
neither impart grave wisdom
they've simply come to visit
these old friends
this family
old wars and wounds forgotten
they bring memories
like loaves and fishes
offered to the starving and bereft
magick lives deep in every root
that reaches unending
tangles present, past, future
into a single skein
our stories bleed like autumn
into every scarlet leaf
that soon falls to leafmeal
making a sweet incense of death
to rise in smoke and solace

we sit about the fire
and warm ourselves
in recollection
hold holy every word
gone too soon
each syllable tolls hollow
its solitary note
melancholy on the wind.

## In which I am *An Cailleach Bhéara**

I don't know when winter became my home,
nor when the sun first failed to renew,
when the owl cast its shadow across my heart,
and the first blossom withered in my hand,
the first child looked away,
and the first crow called my name;

nor when skin, once firm as a grape,
grew raisined, and veins once hidden
began to mark my hands like tributaries,
that guide the ancient power of what I am become
outward to the Great Grey Invisible
that weaves what is and will be.
I don't know when
my words first shaped air into flesh,
when stars first bloomed from my fingers,
and I first bent light into being,
when maiden became most ancient crone,
and fell to the grief of wisdom.

Some nights, there is no sleep;
such times my eyes pierce
the icy curtain that hangs beyond,
and it opens momentarily,
reveals a restless panorama:
visceral dreams recount a maidentime,
when I was new and fair,
each random, rambling love of my libertine life.
They float unreachable now,
trapped in the awful and fluorescent light of memory –
this unwanted perusal of what could not be
and never really was –
each hope that unfeathered fell
to lie piteous on the damp and funereal earth.
It went so quickly,
lost in a kaleidoscope of years.

And in lieu of lovers,
I took on power,
wove the world on a charm,
sprung fresh from the root of sorrow.

I don't know when
I grew so old,
how old I really am.

Go into my attic, Father Pádraig –
count the bones
you find sequestered there.
Let them tell my age –
read scribed upon them
a litany of sins.
Mete me no penance, Father:
I confess only to myself,
and my tears fall stones
enough to build a cairn.

Then get me to the river before sunrise,
before the first lark sings,
and while the hound lies sleeping.
Let me renew;
let me once more recall
the way my body felt
with morning in it.

*An Cailleach Bhéara is Goddess of Creation in Irish myth. She is most ancient of beings. Some stories say that when she grows very old, if she can make it to the river to renew before she hears a dog bark, she will be made young again. It is a winter/spring or death/resurrection myth. There is a story of a priest – some say St. Patrick – who found her and demanded to know her age. She told him to go to the attic and count the bones he found there, remnants of things she'd eaten over millennia. When he returned from the attic, he found her changed, a young woman in her place. Her sister Goddess is Brighid, the Healer. As I grow older, I find there is in all elder women a young woman, still. My reflection always surprises me. And in that sense, I think we all become An Cailleach Bhéara.

# For Charlie at Samhain

You who have been gone
since I was fifteen
how is it that some nights
dreams spin you back
unfasten reality
cut a shining swath
through manypoppied fields that lie
between my staunch four poster
and that netherwhere
no room contains

I feel you clasp my hand
fold it small and safe
within your own
and for those moments
we walk together
yet alone
through a silence of stars

Why should I believe
that your defiance
would not conquer death
that your words
a language of crows
mysterious and strange
would not send a siren call
from those shores
of purple shadows
we so briefly glimpse
while sleeping

Those nights I wake
my room afloat
in a fragrance of lilies
those nights I know myself
not quite alone.

# Price

This is for those whose
glass slipper was a bad fit,
whose compass needle spun awry,
whose breadcrumbs were gobbled by jays,
whose crow flew a crooked path.

And this is for those
whose JiminyCricket sang off-key,
whose prince never arrived,
whose ship never came in,
pot never boiled,
last match guttered out
against the killing snow;
and this is for those
whose golden egg
still hides somewhere in the dark
never to see an Easter morn.

This is for those
unpolished, unadorned,
broken and bent,
doors slammed on fingers;
whose children dance on sidewalk cracks.

It's for those
whose disappointments mask
the garden and the grandeur
of the elemental everyday,
so easily forgotten in pursuit:

Now while the croc's most dread tick-tock
echoes ever closer from behind,
let us embrace the ragged child,
the tattered real,
the broken life;

and open our eyes
to that which is,
seize the ordinary
in empty, grateful hands –
the humble stone, the dormant seed,
the grey, habitual light of day,
the unremarkable weed.

*Can we not learn*
*to cherish these,*
*open our hearts,*
*and cradle inside*
*these gifts neglected*
*and long denied?*

*Someday when asked*
*for our final fare*
*to cross the river*
*as all must dare*
*these golden coins*
*magnificent and rare*
*may pay the boatman*
*waiting there.*

# Flight Risk
*for Barbara*

Impossible flight
unaware that you can't
soar in the light
you hold your own
with petal-winged wonders
in their gossamer lace
never once blunder
keep pace with the skydancing throng
never glance
into an unkind mirror
see your body all wrong
dark and bumbling
never know yourself
a flight risk
never hear the Queen proclaim
your wings inadequate
or a gang of drones on the corner
call you names – say you're bottom heavy
you dance anyhow
in oblivious absurdity
fly anyhow
dive and dip
to sip sweet nectar anyhow
hiving your honey away
unintentional gardener
spreading pollen
stamen to pistil
you accidentally make the world
bloom.

## Morning at the Bird Woman's House

Early coffee on my porch
dawn rises roseate
on eyes still heavy with sleep
birds sense winter stirring
in this chill and early air
shy as children afraid to take a candy
they fly about my feeders

fear landing
chatter to each other
they size me up
decide where I fit in
how much to dare

Something sad and Edenlost
bars the gate between us
scarred by less benign encounters
they fear my kind
grandfathered memories
of slingshots that shatter
the hollowboned like glass
wisdom handed down
feather by feather
they know

I call to them in baby talk
hope to set the record straight
I want to be the woman they can trust
patient
still
I wait an hour
a young titmouse, emboldened
dives down
lights a fractional second
swoops back to the cherry
filled now with the awestruck
community of chickadees and jays
chirping in wonder
he's proud of himself
and he's started something
now they swoop, flit, fly
timid about the feeders
but closer
each time
closer
to this benevolent beast.

# To a leaf

I see your fall
and raise you
up in praise.
I thank you
for the knotted branch,
pregnant with spring,
from which you first emerged,
your early bud
gold as Frost's first green.
You unfolded dear as any blossom
to dance on April breezes,
or make dappledrowsy shadows
across summer's lazy hammock,
where I napped in late July,
until the north wind came
and played another tune,
and you blushed red with autumn;
now released at last,
I see you pirouette
against a late November sky,
and know the branch you left behind
will bear you yet again
when March arrives.

# Contemplation at Lughnasadh

It is the eve of Lughnasadh
and harvest thoughts come easy
what we've planted
what brought forth
for better or for worse

A glamor of a day
heavenskied and golden
Brother Wind blows brisk
and unexpected for the last of July
it rustles through my thoughts
shifts them around
they tumble down
like early spent maple leaves

A ruby throat darts in and out
French kisses columbine
enjoys its honey'd feast
knows what it is
what to expect of its brief time
follows its inner river
toward the inevitable sea
stays with the script, unknowing
miniscule its brain must be
yet smarter still than most of us
like me

who swam against the current
straight for the siren noise
of hormones singing wild
compelling toward rocks irresistible
seduced, I want to say
but cannot abdicate that way
one look and I was lost

in sugared dreams of nurseries
plump babies
eyes empty as dawnsky
fingers that curled, endearing
guileless smiles that swallowed whole
my heart and commonsense

And now the season ends
this field more barren
than it began
desolate, abandoned
left behind
these futile years spent
all in vain
while others gather in
abundance of reward
and sit beside their hearths
fulfilled and blest, content
with family circled round
as for myself
I see it clear
there is no harvest
here.

## Enough

It is never enough.

The hummers
who sip the last of nectar'd day
know this
and leave their regrets for night
on wings that buzz like a fly.

It is never enough.

Not the breeze
that breathed relief
through summer heat
and was gone too soon,

bearing with it the ephemeral scent
of honeysuckle June,
as she wove her magick
in and out
through country fences;

Not the blossom that crept,
wild and unexpectedly scarlet,
into your pristine garden –
how it faded just before
you could share its fine surprise;

Not the music of laughter,
when small arms circled your neck,
as a child stood atop your shoes
while you danced together,
and Buddy Holly sang
through the scratch, pop, hiss
of an old LP;

Not the last bourguignon
your mother made,
taking the recipe
with her into the dark.

Life outlives us,
mayflies all.
That old python,
its coils that grow
ever tighter round our chests
till breath is gone;
our final exhalation
breathes out all we know:

It is never enough.

# Matin

All things praise
as sun retrieves the world
from darkling drear,
there is no sorrow here,
for sad dreams fall away
throughout the
singing / creeping/ chirping / peeping /
hopping / sliding / jumping / gliding
world magnificent,
the plainest creature
busily thankful
in this fair light.

Moth gives thanks that spider missed it,
spider to be ignored by wasp,
wasp that mouse was frightened away,
mouse that it eluded the jay,
jay that cat was occupied,
cat so thankful for frog to chase,
frog is happy to hop and swim,
cricket gives praise for frog hopscotch,
ladybug for cricket oblivious,
(it jumped right over the pebble that hid her),
while aphid says grace for ladybug flight.

All give thanks for life this morning,
for blessing and bliss of sun and rain –
on and on, this matin unending
all the way down the long food chain.

# Vesper

Deep in the gather of dusk,
spirit in me ruffles feathers,
shivers,
nestles in for the night,
wearied from its daylong flight
and ready to find sleep,
along the shores
of straits that flow
twixt seas of dream
and sad reality.

And on return,
no lighthouse marks my flight
nor guides me home,
but dearly recollected acts
of stranger-kindness
from the day:

> *the plain and unaffected smile*
> *the fair word genuine and true*
> *the unexpected, offered hand;*

They shine like pebbles,
white beneath the moon –
and in that light
new hope is born
that gives me will to wake
another morn.

# Conversation with a grasshopper

Namaste,
Friend Grasshopper –
sitting on my doormat,
humble as the old black man,
who used to sell sun-and-earth
tomatoes from his mule-drawn cart
when I was a child.

You look up at me
in beady-eyed wonder,
dwarfed by this looming figure,
my power to crush and destroy
the delicate thorax,
the gossamer wing,
exoskeleton no match
for my size 9s.

Are you puzzled,
as I step over you,
this brush with death?
You jump, but stay,
still staring.

I sit on my covered porch,
sip an evening Shiraz.
Where are my manners?
Should I pour a glass for you?
We are the same, you know,
in many ways.
I am no god –
just taller –
hold no judgement,
care less what Katydid
or didn't do.

Twilight smokes the last rays from the sky;
your brothers sing their autumn song
and die,
yet you have come to visit me;
and I remember
what you were in spring,
pretending to be a leaf,
you greened into the cherry branch,
a fine charade,
a perfect camouflage
to anyone not me.

Now cells grow thick
in every leaf,
the innocence of chlorophyll
lost in a faint blush
that soon bleeds scarlet,
as passion takes each leaf
along the path of destiny
to fall & dance & die.

And where will you hide then,
little friend
so much like me –
I need to know
where will you go
at last?

When we don our final mask
where will we go?

# Leavings

Oh, I've seen summer take her final bow,
seeds pirouette in flight upon each breeze,
bequeath their desperate legacies to spring;
I've seen my careful garden dying down
outside my window; morning glory mouths
are opened wide to catch declining light,
as trees grow silent, ravens prophesy,
cicadas sing like buzz saws, mark the end;
the daughter makes her final dark descent.

And I have seen how autumn takes her leave
in maple somersaults that, earthward bound,
drift down in soundless fall, create incense
of bonfires lit in every smoky lane,
grain ripened, now the sheaves stand tall and gold,
as geese make their departure right on time,
the table groans with harvest; cider press
soon beckons family to hearth and home,
reminding us that we are not alone.

And yet, it's winter's end that moves me most,
for I have seen Death wink at me and flirt
between the nothing promises of limbs
silent, bare and heavy, hung with snow;
I've watched the crocus, fragile as a child,
a liar make of Hades, pierce the ice
to rise victorious in early light,
in brave rebellion shatter arctic crust
to tell us we go on, for so we must.

# Lost

Shaded and sheltered,
consoled by simple things –
spring petals against black bark,
the incense autumn makes –
smell of snow,
verdant moss,
blissful and cool
in summer heat –
children know
these barefoot blessings,
forgotten things,
like dappledawns unending
in which we once believed.

Older now,
we fish in the deepdark,
where memories run
in schools that have survived
whitewater,
sharp rocks,
slow drag of anchors that bind,
irresistible pull of the undertow –
driven to possess
the empty;
we have lost
the ordinary splendor
that was paradise.

# Mama-Teen: The day the music died

I see her dimly
through backdoor memories
the one that hung sideways
on creaking hinges
when I was a child
its manypatched screen
that kept flies out
kept me in

I am seven

Her cherished canary
died this morning
fried to a fritter by August sun
where she'd hung his cage
on the porch
her thought had been
that he needed fresh air

Petey was the only pet
she'd ever had
pride was a sin
and she'd been proud
of owning something
that sang all day
Petey's demise
was clearly the penance
her God had meted out

She never dealt
with guilt so very well
I watch
as she takes down the bowls
measures sugar out
heavy against the feather
on the scale

her tall frame bends
over the kitchen table
red-checkered apron
half un-tied
flour coats her hands
sticks in cracks and crevices
made by age and work and sorrow

She rolls out sweet dough
wraps it in a damp towel to rise
an offering to heal the loss
of Petey and his songs
a tear tracks
through a dust of flour
on her face
she wipes it hastily away
ashamed of this
unmerited release

I follow her to the living room
with its tired lace curtains
and the old piano
carved of dark mahogany
air hangs heavy
smells of Old English furniture polish
and loneliness

I sit beside her on the bench
lean my head against her arm
for comfort
but she recoils
begins to play *You Are My Sunshine*
whispers
*The only music we can keep*
*is what we make ourselves.*

# Bitter end

Crickets sing incessant in her ears
air hangs still, and in the silent roar
she makes her little life alone
through days that dwindle
quickly toward the end
she mental wanders late at night
and in her addled head
she does the things she never did
in places never traveled, never known

her years a coin spent otherwhere
on children who forget her now
on neverending office chores
and midnight mopping floors
and washing grade school uniforms
before she fell asleep
and woke to start again
until she was too old

all gone to babies
gone to pay the bills
she never had enough to pack a bag
take off and find some other place
with yet another life
ashamed to think so selfishly back then

and now, she is abandoned to her fate
regrets the loss of self, when in the end
she's left with nothing but *whatcouldhavebeen*
and wonders at the drunken rage of gods
who warred with equity
contrived this hollow lot
for one who followed all the rules so well
not guessing that her path would lead
to hell.

# Homer the Least

Least Shrew, how dare they name you so,
when you're the most that you can ever be?
I've seen you through a sleepy haze
of morning coffee. Always on the fly,
a dark and smoky blur,
an apologetic skitter across my walk,
one side of the porch to the other,
where you've made your home
beneath the edge of mine.

Tiny. Humble. Black. Other.
Traits that will never make you desirable
in this neighborhood;
but for the record,
I bid you welcome,
dub you Homer the Least,
eater of insects, isopods,
and the bright green tail
formerly the property of Larry the Lizard
who lives beneath the holly –
none of which are any loss to me.
I feel no need to squeal and run,
no revulsion at your silly snout,
no mad desire to crush your fragile bones
beneath a heavy stone or human foot.

Go in peace and meekly on your way;
you make no scar upon the earth or me,
hoping only to be left alone,
taking only what you must to live,
a slug, a centipede, a worm or two,
a drop of water
from my drainpipe now and then,
reminding me
how much I have to learn.

# Writing with Alzheimer's

Did she use up all the words?

an embryonic thought
aborted
before she can form the question

they slip away
(the words)
like water through her fingers
at a holy font
first
a line of poetry
then
what do you call
the thing you put in a lock
to open it

on kinder days
she is simply
otherwhere
those days
she disappears herself
to a void
that doesn't bewilder

at night she dreams
a shoreline
sky starless and black
where words float in
on a lazy tide
opalescent as jellyfish
she reaches for them
finds only seafoam
it dissolves to nothing
she wakens
palms stinging

time is a behemoth
tentacles tangled
with names and faces
sister
daughter
aunt
merge and are lost
in the labyrinthine dark
her grief silent
for what
she can't remember
and trying to
sets her teeth on edge

last night
her mirror shattered
as though to create
a more accurate reflection.

# Little girl lost

Here is the thing I never tell
forged in fires of hell, the secret
chanted to myself
on rosaries of wormwood
in this wilderness I wander
through shifting dapplelight
this ragged path I follow
spirit hollowed out
by memory's scalpel

images unmerciful
ribbons and gummy bears
paper roses
Crayola on manila
blue-speckled eggs
fallen to earth and shattered
how we found them
when she was three
a caterpillar caught by early frost
nothing mattered so much
as wings ended before flight
photos brown and faded
where she stood in the shallows
watching koi in the pool below
how they flashed and flared
through stippleshadow
when sunshafts pierced the indigo
then into the dark again
and though I feared
she never stepped off the ledge
balanced on the edge of things

she grew tall
grew away
flew

yet a solitary darkness
whispered she would fall
for years I lived with hands extended
ready for the catch
but then too late
my arms not long enough
my grip not strong
my heart a thing
rusted shut.

## The way I left Monteagle

Time ticking down
I want to notice
everything before I go
for I am drunk and dazzled
on the nectar of this place
and weary of the dissonance of man
who hawks his wares
and wars against the music
of the natural world

From this bluff
the sunset flares flamboyant
and twilight draws its purple curtains round
so gradually one might not notice
might find herself lost
and wandering this wildwood dark

Yet here I wait
while cooler air drifts down
and dances through tall grass
beside the brook
birds go silent
give way to cricketsong
and the steady tinnital hum of cicada
this little patch of wild purslane
closed up shop an hour ago
petals folded in to wait the sun
now fireflies lift their tiny earthbound stars
and as the bells of Breslin Tower toll
hollow and far away
everything becomes
an evening prayer

Though I must leave
I know beyond the wondering
I'll feel the pull that draws me here again
the way the ocean's yearning moves it tidal
the way sunflowers stretch
stem and petal longing for the light
and on my drive toward home
the way these pines lean after me
longfingered branches
beckoning forever.

# Dinkinesh*

*on a hiking trail in April*

Sun rises
above the ridge
dawn dances
and beneath her flame
of cirrus petticoats
here in the wildwood
shadowstippled dapplelight
shifts rose to gingerlight
a grace of petals drifts
like butterflies
unconscious of the breeze
that carries them
birds stir
wakened by songs
they were dreaming
river murmurs stories
older than stone
there is no need
for language
nothing here can be contained
in syllables
and I know
my heritage.

Three thousand millennia past
Lucy
ancient mother
stood upright and
wonderstruck
reached skyward
toward a scatter of stars.

*Lucy is the most famous fossil of Australopithecus afarensis, a bipedal ancestor of us all, who lived in Ethiopia over 3 million years ago. She got her name from the Beatles' song "Lucy in the sky with diamonds," which was played repeatedly by the team that discovered her. In Ethiopia, she is known as Dinkinesh, which means "you are marvelous" in the Amharic tongue.*

# Make me a Nine

I don't want ten pristine nails to hesitate my fingers
from engaging fertile soil, bringing forth
tomatoes or an April's worth of daffodils
or wiping the snotty nose of a child.

I don't want ten pedicured toes that never knew a blister,
that recoil from barefoot treks up a stone-bruising hill
to watch a flamboyant sun tango with last night's moon.

I don't want to be Bo Derek,
running down a Technicolor beach in her infinite braids
perspiration-free, skinny ass bronzed, waxed legs shining,
unseen orchestra drowning out the sea.

I relish my own perfection, this body disproportionate.

Let me run headlong in my sweat and humanity,
dive into this ramshackle world, arms flung wide,
love fiercely and foolishly, without regret,
feed birds, muck stables, give birth to babies and poems,
dream things I can't possibly live to see.

In this rambunctious, temporary love affair,
let me be intimate with earth before I lie down in it.
Let it scar, stain, tattoo me
with the glory of my identity,
which is perfection by the numbers and the gods.

And in it all, let there be something left
to reach for, hope for, dream for.
In this world of plastic Tens,
make me a Nine.

# The Glassmaker's Son

Lightning struck sand
thus he was born
clearly different
into the world
leaded and stained

into a family of glassmakers
artisans of colour and light
where he alone lived
transparent

no one noticed him
crystalline, brittle
save when sun
made its rare transit

then words
prism'd through him
fractured light into hues
wonderful and strange
that no rose window
could bear

being pellucid
all the more fragile
he disappeared
no one noticed when
chip by
fissure by
fragment
he broke
into shards
splinters
that shatter
those who come near.

# Auld Lang Syne

*a fairytale*

Deepnight, otherwhere and faraway
fireworks Van Gogh'd
inexhaustible heavens
with swirls of stars
that fractured, shattered
a momentary scatter of emberfall
prismed through treetop silhouettes

midnight bells
splintered voices of our friends
lively greeted one another
while evanescent kisses
sprouted glass stiletto'd dreams
in champagne addled heads

beGrimmed by such enchantments
beneath that carnival sky
wayward child
I believed
everafter could be happily now
and such love bloomed so unseasonal
even the mothering earth
embraced me joyful
as false spring
until

fast
fast
that icy stumble down the stairs
the tattered gown
the tangled hair
the broken coach
the fall
brief as pyrotechnic stars

dark
dark
and burning out
skies blacker somehow
more empty
than before.

# Sonnet for an erstwhile prince

Remember how you Cinderella'd me,
and pinned a tinfoil crown into my hair?
And how our castle carpeted with moss
was lit with fireflied lanterns everywhere?

How simple to deceive a springborn child,
eyes dazzledrowned in stars, with paper dreams,
whose secrets have no locks, whose trust, no end,
an innocent romance, not as it seems;

but happily you'd everafter me,
so I believed, as April cast her spell.
And yet the slipper falls, the midnight tolls
for one who loves not wisely and not well.

A briar, a barb, a thorn to pierce the skin,
for once-upon-a-time comes not again.

# Sonnet in retrospect

The lies they tell us when we are too young
to see beyond the stars that crowd our eyes,
bedecked in roses, ribbons, they're disguised
like sugar in foul medicine, a trick.

The speckles on the leaf that mark the end
of fragile garden plants, the bud gone brown,
the jaw gone slack, the happy sun gone down:
they tell another tale we fail to see

until it is too late, we've swallowed whole
the bitter pill, the gate has rusted closed;
the truth that might have saved us, if disclosed –
yet grasping fairytales, we chose to love.

How wise are they who never play the fool
who wade the safer shallows of the pool.

# The Last Magick

You were the last magick

*gone* – with all out-of-season things
last rose in winter
final swallowtail stilled by frost
last hummer at an ice-coated pane

*one* – with things that go too quickly
cotton candy on the tongue
momentary thrill of taking a hill too fast
that brief falling sensation
that makes you gasp

*meaningless* – like other things I put too much stock in
last song I'm thinking of
suddenly playing on the radio
last person I dreamed about
ringing me up

*gone* – with all my brittle omens
first star, found penny
cricket on the hearth
clover, wishbone
bluebird feather, rabbit foot

*one* – with harbingers of grief
blue-eyed candle flame, bird trapped indoors
shattered photograph, stopped clock
chill up my spine, crow's caw
hat on the bed.

# December, Gethsemane

The long descent of winter has begun,
nests of summer birds ice sculptured now,
I see their gelid glitter amongst vines
once verdant, now shriveled grey with cold.
The mirror tells me Youth fled long ago,
her ribbons flying wild upon the wind
unfettered now, jesses broken free,
gone she is, with all her April dreams,
her secret hopes plowed-under;
they fed no resurrecting spring,
and only stubble fields remain,
lit amber here,
beneath a dying sun.

It's truly done, I think.
This garden's bleak remains
hold only torment
through an endless night,
where comrades sleep,
oblivious and blind
to tears wrung bloody
from a thorn-pressed heart,
and silver-bartered kisses
that recall far memories
of vinegar and gall,
the bootless plea
against the force-fed cup,
and how the hour of crosses
goes burning in the skull
toward cock-crowed denial
and inevitable dawn,
the grey sun rising,
no horizon.

## Winter apocalypse

There is no Rosetta Stone
to translate the wreckage
strewn in this late winter's swollen wake
grief is a garbled tongue

nothing turns
to words pronounceable
these fateful runes
woven double helix
these legacies of the flesh we suffer
stand imperfect as our lives

death has moved among us
a dancer
fingers slender and pale

snatch this one and that
it penetrates the surface of complacence
and we no longer feel assured
of anything, save our mortality

our fragile lives that stir like dust
upon the fickle breath of gods
or burn like pages of books on Kristallnacht
their wisdom rising
in a chimney of ash and air
like wings
like angels
all we have written
brought to nothing

oblivious, we dangle
from Odin's tree
cling to each other
ephemeral as mayflies
we grasp
as though they belong to us
these indefinite years.

# Cherry-on-Top

Cherry-on-Top
drove a new '63 VW
Pepto Bismol pink just like her
lipstick and leather miniskirt
Maybelline eyes
cantaloupe breasts
stood out
in our flat-chested reality
sunny-haired blue-eyed
running on empty
Cherry was the sure thing
cheerleading future wife
of a quarterback
envy of underlings

*acne'd adolescent*
*whispers of pot and blow*
*jobs at away-games*
*sneaking under bleachers*
*Spanish Fly*
*by night Boones Farm*
*sticky sweet cherry-*
*flavoured four-letter words*
*giggled secrets, lies and gossip*
*her nickname a joke*
*in every locker room*

Cherry-on-Top driving by
in perfect pink oblivion
decades gone
Cherry-on-Top sells
patterns at Justine's Fabrics
proud moms of new cheerleaders
scoop them up

one breast
and crowning glory
gone to cancer
cherry scented lipstick
stains creep into lines
hard around Cherry lips
eyeliner dragged in
jagged marks across
crepe paper lids

Cherry says
how she remembers
when she was on top
complete with rhinestone tiara
pink orchid corsage so big
she couldn't look down
to see us wave
when she was queen
and how the gym
decorated in tissue paper
chicken wire and
christmas lights
looked just like
heaven must.

# Fear God / Love God

*There is no fear in love, but perfect love casts out fear. For fear has to do with punishment, and he who fears is not perfected in love. — 1 John 4:18*

## I: Fear God

That bogeyman we made
Who skulks about like a warden
checking bed sheets for semen stains
or examining fingers for the presence of a ring
tallying up the score on His naughty-or-nice list
counting fibs and blaming ribs added or taken away
snickering as He cuts notches on His gun
each time a soldier falls in wars over what to call Him
giving extra credit for the lopping off of hands
when the hungry steal a loaf of bread
listening for the vain or misspoken Name
clucking His tongue when a knee bends
to scrub a floor instead of praying at a Sunday altar
that name-taker God who frowns if we tell a white lie
to compliment an unattractive neighbor
or if we're jealous of another's lavish begonias
fear that God who lets tyrants slaughter innocents
and chalks it up to free will

Oh fear that black-winged God
with His fiery eyes and His frigid heart
who locks the doors of Heaven
against the humanity of humans
yet presses His nose against our windows
like a covetous child.

## II: Love God

That one we knew as children but forgot
Who was lost in books other people wrote
that God who laughs in a shower of blossoms
and plays peek-a-boo with babies who can still see Her
making them giggle helpless when we see nothing there
that God who dazzles rainbows from heaven's prism
and proudly tacks up our crayon drawings on His ceiling
gazing at them with a Parent's eyes
Who is patient when we fall and sends angels to prop us up
Who sends spring when our hearts can't bear another snowfall
Who weeps with our sorrows
Who feeds with manna the starving soul
Who knows our names and loves without condition
that God who stays our hand
when we would stone another for the same desires we hold
Who doesn't care what name we call Her
or whether we count Her male or female
that God who blows out the matches we keep playing with
and still believes we can do better

Oh love that bright-winged God
with His shining face and Her open heart
love Him to distraction; love Her with your whole being
Who opens wide the doors of heaven
Who presses His nose against our windows
like a Mother watching over Her brood.

# For Charlie in the afterwhere

*7 January 2015*

I send you this poem
this little orphan
threadbare and huddled in alleyways
sleeping on park benches in my head
for over a week now
like some cast member from *Les Mis*
hiding its face
and dodging the cops
who would roust it out
in favor of something
more well-dressed
to speak in eulogy

but you lived stark naked
you were all muscle
fearless foot-to-the-crotch assault
on those who begged for it
for years you plowed
acres of acrimony
like Swift with brassier balls
you just put it out there
and waited for the weekly detonation
now religious morons
follow dictates of imaginary playmates
and twelve disciples fall
martyred

So this rough little bastard
with its tropeless lines
words burlapped and knotted
seems more appropriate
I hope you never rest in peace
I hope you haunt every word and sketch
defy
offend

shock
provoke
right-wing sheep
and brainless zealots
I hope someday
the world shouts as one
eyes and minds wide open
understanding what they claim
*Je suis Charlie!*

# Survivor's Guilt

Nights I can't sleep
my mind writes letters to you
in the dark
words morning will erase
in a fresh wash of light
I share myself
casual as a mint
intimate stories
one might offer
to a fellow passenger
on a plane
someone you'll never see again

sometimes
you break through the surface
of my dreams
a shark
sensing blood

sometimes
I review those final years
your memory browning out
your world
insubstantial as cardboard
I picture your face
mannequin calm
blessedly oblivious
at the end
you didn't even know
my name

some nights I wonder
if you remember me in afterwhere
beside some indolent sea
tideless and without life
skies unbroken by flight

on those nights
I wake panicked
my covers twisted
into a hangman's noose.

## Children
*a divorce settlement*

Deep in the firestorm of autumn
we planted daffodils
bulbs that cloistered vague ideas
of perennial springs
and gardens yet unborn
we kissed them for luck
blanketed them with mulch
and told them bedtime stories
to send them dreaming
soft and drowsy
into the long nap to come

Snow came
and ice
we grew dull and distant
old and numb
all feeling gone
you went away
or I left
whatever story
suits the memory today
whatever makes it
easier to take

Yet now beneath a liliaceous sky
all laced with brilliant redbuds overhead
I drive past our old house
and find these sunny petals
trumpeting new life
and I know
regardless of the guilt
beside the pain
the bitter gall
of dark regret
the stain that soils
those many years
the frigid winters
absent springs
in truth
we never lost a thing.

# Bramble

When Bramble was three
her stepfather threw her
from the front porch
into Grandmother's roses
late that night
she felt a bump
under the wounded skin
on her chest
and a sting
sharp and insistent

Something had taken root
just beneath the surface
it hurt at first
but being so young
and without words
that could be hung together and shared
with someone who could help
she got used to it

When Bramble was seven
Stepfather Two showed her
what bad touch meant
and that night
as she wept
beneath her covers
confused by twisted dreams
the something emerged
black and sharp and shiny
like a thorn
it calmed her
became her secret
quiet and perfect
hidden carefully
beneath t-shirts

and pinafores
better, she thought
that it didn't show

When Bramble's mother was beaten
by Stepfather Three
and left for dead
in a cardboard crate
on the back porch
a dozen thorns
popped up beside the first
and so it went
thorn after thorn
a thriving garden of them

In junior high
when she was bullied
left bloody on the shower room floor
a long brown stem of them
wrapped in a tangle
about her body
pointed sides outward
soft as velvet
against her skin

Within this strange armor
no one could ever touch her
no one would even try
and as time passed
the thorns grew thick with age
and strong
nothing could break them
not to hurt
not to hug
not to heal
an angel
sheathed in barbed wire

cocooned
and safe
and alone

When Bramble died
they found no letter to explain
they found her naked
in her Grandmother's garden
saw at last
how she was cloaked in thorns
how she was crowned by them
how her blood bloomed now
red and royal
from her palms
like roses.

# Advent

Rainsong comes sweeping
on westerwinds
puddlelicious with April
clumsy flower girl
who strews the world
with small delights
of newly lacquered leaves
and blue-eyed blossoms
blessing all of humankind
even those who refuse to bow
to Gaia anymore
yet truth catches in the throat
of every lily
floats upon the song
of every bird
and the most shriveled soul
finds a spare room left
to lay a grudging altar
to what needs not belief
but simply
is.

# Kitchen witch

Mom's kitchen was an office
with an old Olivetti for an oven
where she cooked up
the occasional spell
for clients with enough green
to make her magick worthwhile
as she conjured ad campaigns
that made noxious perfume irresistible
turned torturous stilettos into objects of desire
or PR initiatives
that turned straw to gold, toads to princes
made the Emperor see clothes as entirely optional
and the wealthy crave the ridiculous

My grandmother dared knock once
to remind her of my violin recital
the poor woman fled, pale and shaken
never to interrupt again
leaving Mom alone
to churn out hot concepts
never cookie cutter
never sweet

Like the lily I gave her on Mother's Day
that languished for lack of attention
just beyond the window's light.

# Deception

In the fireflied childhood of my life
wildwood where I ran feral and unfettered
in the white pearl morningworld
I gloried in each liliaceous sky
in borning rays of rising sun
unwary of what comes
that flesh declines, and in the deepnight
even brightest stars refuse to shine
their light invisible to eyes
whose sweetest joy has soured to sorrow
that what is made this day in paradise
can be destroyed tomorrow and
buried close beneath the newborn face
so graceless and impatient wait
void-eyed skull and polished bone
that twilight comes, the strongest fail
and quite alone we finally bed down
a deathwatch of our ghostly forebears
gathered round to mock
or that the blackrobed cart
thunders close behind
its ominous vibrations jar
grind spirit, mind and joints
sick secret hidden as an appleworm
in swaddling clothes of every foundling babe
and through soulcaverns, death howls
hungry as the owl that seeks its prey
or that we all must fall to ash someday.

## womanpoem

There was a woman at the edge of the forest
and she was singing songs
she was singing songs
to the earth that opened itself to bring forth life
as she did
songs
to the moon that waxed and waned in its cycle
as she did
songs
to the waters that ebbed, that flowed
as she did
and she sang down fire
she sang the winds from their four towers
she sang till the earth quickened
beneath her dancing feet
and water poured forth from the listening stones
*and something older than morning*
*heard*

and something was borning
in the burning shadows
in the singing silence that fell between her words
in the dawning of that darkness

There was a woman at the edge of the forest
and she was calling down power
she was calling down power
from the womangods
power
in all its ancient names
Ishtar, Isis, Demeter, Hecate
power
calling on chaos to bring the order
power
calling on madness to give birth to reason
power

till the scales could balance once more
*and something older than sunrise*
*heard its unspeakable name*

There was a woman at the edge of the forest
and she was cursing the things
that blackened the soul of earth
cursing
war and avarice and violence
cursing
marketplace manlogic
cursing
the rape of the Mother
and she was invoking
an older order
a wiser way
a womanpath
and something was borning
in the burning shadows
in the singing silence that fell between her words
in the dawning of that darkness

There was a woman at the edge of the forest
and she was weaving womanstories
she was weaving womanstories
like spiderwebs
and the light fell clinging silver to the words
stories
of the power of the daughters
who birthed and taught and nurtured men
men who ruled to ruin
stories of strength
stories of the source of all
of the daughters
of the Mother
abused
bruised

battered by the power of the manworld
which is brutality
which is war
which is the power of the marketplace
*and something older than death*
*rose up angry*

There was a woman at the edge of the forest
and she was singing down the power
she was naked
her hair was wild and singed
and she smelled of fire
because she had walked through the center
because no one circumnavigates hell
she had brought forth
pomegranates for the daughters
and laurels to crown them
she had brought forth a new way
she told them of their Mother
and that their time is beginning

and something was borning
in the burning shadows
in the singing silence that fell between her words
in the dawning of that darkness

*and something older than birth*
*opened its arms in welcome.*

## Crone's counsel
*or how to see in a spring forest*

Go deep
into the wild
where no one has bruised the earth
where nothing is opaque
and everything you need to know
lies sleeping just below the surface

leave the hounds that trouble you
to bay outside in futility
where we are going
they cannot follow
bring what hurts you here
find a stump or stone
sit and be patient

soon your eyes will adjust
and you will see
how in this darkness
of wood and fern
dogwood petals float
effortless and pale
impossible as phantoms
as though they are attached to nothing
of this earth
for them there is no gravity

see those tiny mushrooms
gathered in a fairy ring
and know they have waited
all this time tender and fragile
they have survived
for this moment
for you alone to see them

notice these tiny forget-me-nots
how even they are important
how they thrive blue and strong
and outnumber giant trees
that rise above them

now listen
the birds know you have come
and sing your welcome
thank them

the wind whispers your name
in a new language
learn it
let fear drop away
and hesitation evaporate
more swift than morning dew
make a truce with yourself
breathe

let everything bloom
that was seeded inside you long ago
and when you leave this place
you will find the hounds have gone
to seek another quarry.

# For Kit

When I first met Kit,
she was crouched behind a streetlight
stealing lives with her camera.
Feral and free, she didn't belong here
any more than I did –
she tousled the hair of public opinion
as though it were a wayward child,
forgivable in its ignorance, and a little silly.

Each portrait, a double-edged razor –
nude photos of socially prominent women.
The Ladies' Art Council minced no words:
*That dawg don't hunt here.*

Cheeky bitch, she got under the skin
and into the head,
made people squirm –
especially when a city councilman
discovered his Father's Day surprise:
expectant wife and two adolescent daughters
immortalized *au naturel* in a local gallery –
and then there was a judge's aging wife,
naked save for her pipe,
smoke wafting upward,
she sat on a velvet chair,
legs judiciously crossed,
fearless gaze dead-on,
into the lens.

One day, Kit tired of it all,
the taunts, the blatant jealousy,
from dimestore photographers and the Christian Family League.
Gypsy scarf peeking out beneath her biker helmet,
she left us in her rearview mirror,
watched us all grow smaller
with her departure.

# The beautiful dead

The beautiful dead visit us in dreams
glide through the veil weightless
mum as lilies
they keep their own counsel
no lexicon in common with us anymore
the beautiful dead are indifferent to our apologies
though we try to express our regret
and our deep embarrassment
that we have survived them
they do not say, *There, there* or try to touch
they stand still as icons
awkward as wallflowers at the spring dance
not knowing what to do with their hands
or as one might sit in a waiting room
counting the seconds
till their name is called in a new language
and their sentence is up

Therefore let us not summon them
from their new world
rather let us lay them down
in sweet spring meadows of our souls
and when winds of turmoil
swirl about our lives
and trouble the blossoms there
the beautiful dead shall stir
and memories rise
a comforting fragrance
we can't quite name
but know their presence
embraces us
as best they can.

## The one

I am the one you have feared
since air burned your lungs
with that first borning breath
I am the shadow that rocked your cradle
humming lullabies in a minor key

I am the pea beneath your mattress
gobbler of bread crumb trails
frost on the match girl's fingers
the ticking crocodile
I am the one who arsenics the apple
hexes the spindle
haunts the sleepless hollows of your mind

I am the Great Fee Fi Fo Fum

I curdle the milk
stop the clock
cause the rooster to crow at midnight

I am the one who owns the big black dog

I am the one who
weighs the sum of everything
against a feather
legacy of the garden
curse of the garnet seeds

I am the boatman's boss

Though you run five miles a day
and eat only parsley
I will find you
though you stack chairs against the door
and hide beneath the covers

I will have my way
prayers and chants and charms
and all your ragged little gods
cannot protect you

Comes the day we meet
you will laugh at your folly
for you will find I am also
merely a pit stop
on the infinite path.

# Growing up with a lunatic

My stepfather was psychotic
and I grew up knowing
about watched pots
and the fallacy around them
ever vigilant
I knew
all about boiling points

One morning
we'd be civil
dine on oranges
and coffee from Seville
he'd lecture us on manners
tell us how beautiful we were
then play the old Steinway
order me to sing
*Someone to watch over me*
and I would
trembling
the ribbons in my hair
less adornments
than a falcon's jess
tethered to a role
I had to play

Another day
he'd speak of how ugly I was
how he'd like to tattoo my skin
with a hot poker
brand me with cigarettes

Or how easy it would be for him
to drown my siblings
in the stream behind our house
while I slept unaware

how he could bury them all
beneath the cool mosses
and I'd only have myself
to blame

Some nights I'd waken
my mouth filled with blood
from chewing my tongue

I left long ago
flew
jesses trailing on the wind
yet no one ever gets away
entirely

an old woman now
there are mornings
I put ribbons in my hair
sit on my porch
and sing
*Someone to watch over me*
for no good reason.

# Hesitation

In that soundless moment
when angels of inspiration
waft in from otherwhere
to breathe their blessings upon us
encircle us with strong arms
then wing up and away
leaving us
to our own divinity

in that vestal millisecond
just before we accept
the crossroads bargain
sign that ironclad contract
just before the moment
we can't take back

before we set first foot
on fresh snowfall
or lie with a fertile lover
before we violate blank canvas
with the first bleeding stroke of paint
place the first note
on the empty staff
type the first word
on the unblemished page

let us remember our history
how it all turned out before
how the Maker saw the downfall
from innocence to menace
serpent to bloody brother
Auschwitz to Darfur
let us recall the Sorcerer's Apprentice
how not much good can come
from dabbling in the arts

then let us exhale
gird up our loins
stand our ground
spoil the snow
bear the bastard child
paint the masterwork
write the symphony
pen the poem
and because it is inevitable
lose the garden
with a measure of joy.

# Bitch

Whatever poison runs through the veins of wolves
that draws them to some solitary place,
there to howl in altercation
with the moon,
runs burning through my veins tonight,
and restless,
sweating,
I rise and pace
this carpeted wilderness,
these rooms grown strange.

How many times have we mated
on nights like this,
rain beating
like the frantic hands of a jealous wife
against the windows?
How many nights have you fed my craving,
a mad thing
wild and tangled
with tears and earth
come crying in from the woods?
How many years have I let you hide
your anger and your grief inside me?
I have learned so well how easily
one passion is spent in another.
And is this love
that gorges itself,
then slips to some cave apart
and gnaws the bones of memory,
till it grows lean and hungry
once more?

I write this under a hunter's moon,
the years baying behind me
like a pack of hounds.

# Bliss

Some things you can't look at
can't look away from
can't get out of your head
stopped at a traffic light
I look down

black and white and bleeding out
a small cat lies
already dead
and doesn't know it
golden bell about her neck
jingles with every move
she had belonged
to someone

she washes her face
genetically instructed
to perform this final act
of macabre grooming
pink tongue licking
pink paws stroking
she purrs a death rattle
ignorant of the inevitable
numb to life
blooming out of her

looking into green eyes glazing over
you'd hardly notice hind quarters severed
legs tossed casually onto the median
or how the gutter runs crimson now

*some things you can't get rid of*
*even after all those years*
*as you fasten my necklace*
*as I straighten your tie*
*I hear her purr.*

# Medusa

It's not as though I was the first
to trade my shining curls for coils
or follicles for fangs
to share a taste
for all things wise and serpentine
after all, it was your Eve
who dared the Knowledge Tree
with its ripe fruit
she, too, was faced
with all the hair-brained
myths men make
when they can't reconcile
a woman's beauty
with a well-endowed IQ
the same as those
who claim that I was cursed
when truthfully, this stunning coif
is shrewd Athena's gift
these slithering dreads that petrify
yet turn men soft
where it counts most to them
my friends here threaten none
though I'll admit
a cowlick now and then
when it's deserved
and as for Freud
there's little phallic
to be found in women's wisdom.

Beware, beware
my lovely face
my writhing hair
but know each night
these serpent fangs

sink deep into my brain
there to impart
sweet venom
bitter knowledge
of men with flaccid will
and stony heart.

# Lilith

Who I am sneaks up on a man
though I can tell when he knows
by his nervous laugh
or the way he can't quite focus
on things like the stock market
or football scores
that infinitely pleasurable moment
when I know he's lost control

I never know
just what may tip him off
the candles at the bottom of the stairs
always burning
though no one lights them
or the shadow of a lion
that prowls across the wall
perhaps, it's that ill wind
howling clear and cold
around the eaves
though it's hot August
and not a leaf is stirring
more often, it's those pale fingers
that trace words on the wainscoting
after dinner:  *mene mene tekel* . . .

Along about then he realizes
I didn't come from any man's rib
and I'm no Eve
who needs a snake to tell her
what to do
hell, I planted the tree he crawled out of

I sing up tsunamis, baby
take your children
steal your soul
fuck with your dreams.

# Circe

Transforming men to swine was not a stretch;
I barely had to put the kettle on.
For inside every man, there lives a letch,
and each of them is far less brain than brawn.

There was no spell, no chant, no cauldron stirred;
I just suggested strolling on the shore.
One glance at my four nymphs, no magic word,
the switch was made, and they were men no more.

To tell the truth, I do regret this deed,
although I found it humorous at first;
their appetites incessant I must feed,
and now it's I who find myself accursed.

# Magdalen

And who was I, that I should love a god?
A woman made of earth and warm desire,
who in his dusty footsteps humbly trod
a pace behind, yet stoked the gossips' fire

with my mere presence. I was ever mute
when questioned by disciples at his side,
and jealous of his favor, they'd dispute
my right to his affection. They denied

the place I never felt I truly owned.
Though still, when angels rolled away the stone
that early Easter morning, he chose me
to witness first his stunning victory.

Yet be it miracle, or be it art,
his *noli me tangere* crushed my heart.

# Trial

*For the legions of women slaughtered and defamed in the name of God.*

Those hard commandments placed in human hands,
appropriately carved upon a stone,
provoke the worst in those who are inclined
to punish what they cannot understand.
And so it was that I stood there at last
before the temple courts in Galilee.

I felt no shame before these Pharisees
who dragged me from my sweet beloved's bed
into the blinding light and choking dust,
nor that they shoved me naked, ridiculed
before a crowd that lusted for revenge
against a woman who had only done
what they did every night within their dreams.
And yet I felt such shame to be a pawn
to snare a man more innocent than I.

They put the question to him clear and plain:
In Moses' name, should they not stone me now?

I saw him bent and writing in the dust,
each mark undoing what the tablets said,
each mark unwinding every tangled word,
each mark replacing punishment with grace.
Then finally he spoke his fair reply:
that he without a sin should cast the first.

I watched them drop their stones and walk away,
all seething at this man's audacity,
and yet still struck with wonder at his words.
I waited there to gather up the stones,
I took them home and made of them a cairn.

# Way of the Raven

Skylarks never contemplated
benefits of asphalt
flown to shrinking woodlands
they compose hymns
of loss and longing
to Gaia

Ravens are another matter
appreciating occasional
squirrel meets Goodrich
or hare outfoxed
by Volkswagen

Nevermore crows
scavenge amongst tall grasses
remove that which fouls
sweet country air
but congregate
along this highway
raspy caws announcing
smoggy dawn
they leisurely await
the next convenient kill

Nor can we blame these
bold opportunists
who make the best
of progress
our fast food delivery
of carrion
we too lazy to walk
whose faith lies
in the Mórrígan
sprawling cities

that feed her warlords
highways between
that carry us
swift-commuting
angels of death
delivering our message of
doom to chipmunk
hapless armadillo
and homeless lark

On weekends
making our escape
to the country
see them swagger
off the median
like they own the place
Hitchcock their heads
peer into windows
of cars stopped at red lights
take our measure
dream of bigger game.

# Letter from Eve

When earth was young and greening
before I leapt from the Garden
to walk the world outside
first and unfettered
I conversed with serpents
and tasted their seedy fruit
then sealed them
with the print of my heel
upon their heads
and split their tongues
to confound their language
that they might not prey
upon my children

I did the best I could
with my own
yet when my son
took the life of his brother
and fertilized the fields with blood
I understood
the forbidden was never
a sacred Knowledge
of art or healing
but of violence and death
that old appleworm

All those I bore
and those they bore
perished
but I was Original Woman
sprung from the Garden
immortal
such is the weight of my curse
to live on
as stone and light, as water
and one with all that grows

thus, I watched
my legacy unfold

So it was I
who comforted you
in your mother's womb
it was my voice
that sang you lullabies
to the ticking rhythm
of her metronome heart
and it was I who wrote
the myths that filled your head
to explain me

I watched you stand
rise from the muck
and right yourself on two legs
saw how easily
you were broken
and moved by your fragility
I gave you every vegetable thing
you needed to survive

And knowing that any god
had abandoned us long ago
like any single mother
I watched you reach
for my invisible self
applauded your ambition
saw you discover
the round world
even launch yourselves
into space to seek answers
among the stars
yet all the while
I was in front of you
in every stone, root and petal
yet you were blind to me

Serpent song
that old infection
rose in you
and I watched you tug at threads
unravel and unpin
the fabric of life
saw you spin the double helix
like a roulette wheel
saw you plunder my treasures
to slay by fusion and fission
tear at the building blocks
of your precarious world
fell woodlands
pollute oceans
mutate that which grew
pure and perfect

Yet still I fed you
allowed you
to suck at my breasts
until only blood came forth
for I have loved you

Now I am old and wearied
within me storms whip
through canyons
where once flowed
long-ago rivers and streams
where once crops blessed fecund earth
and once thrived
forest, fin and feather
now there are only desert places
where winds howl
and with sand inscribe
upon my ribs
rune-written prophecies
that no one deciphers.

# Are you scared yet?

Drifting over Eden
in this dark, ill-chosen hour
do you glance below
and see the shadows?

now that the oily wake of the rigs
suffocates bird and beast
now that it wanders its noxious path
through fertile wetlands
destroys future generations
smears flower, feather, reed

now that Wall Street's anointed
offer up unctuous cash
as though it will purchase back
all things winged and wondrous
and those that swam free
between the great coral ribs
of the mother

claw and fang are impotent
against this malignancy
and boats of hungry fishermen
a poor defense
against this vile armada

across the bayou
the hollow lament of mission bells
prays without words.

# Don't tell Mama

what we've done here
if she finds out
oh man
she's gonna be pissed

we were just playing
having a good time
and now just look at what we've done

oh man
look at the mess we've made
of her garden

oh man
look at how her pets died
starting with the birds
and now even the bees are leaving

oh man
look at how we made everything so dirty
with our toys
how the streams
look like a backed-up toilet
how the air
burns our eyes
how we've even broken
her thermostat

oh man
there may not be time to clean this up
no time to fix things
before she sees

oh man
she's gonna be mad

*hey*
*do you think she knows already?*
*was that an earthquake*
*or was that her*
*shaking with rage?*
*was that a tornado*
*or was that her*
*getting ready*
*to clean house?*
*was that a tsunami?*
*or was that her*
*warming up*
*to give us the whipping of our lives?*

*oh man*
*Mama's coming*
*and she's pissed.*

# Don't tell the children

Don't tell them
how we ate snow ice cream
free of factory made contamination
piggybacked poison
with the snowfall

Don't tell them
how we drank from virgin streams
unsullied by our greed
how we swam crystalline waters
clear as our consciences

Don't tell them
how we picked blackberries
in the wild
let juice drip down our chins
without a toxic thought
how we climbed orchard trees
to steal unwashed cherries

Don't tell them
how we hiked untouched glory
watched a thousand suns set
in rainbowed splendor
unenhanced by airborne chemicals
that alter nature's palette
and photoshop our view

Don't let them know
about brightfeathered wonders
and Amazonian treasures
lost to marketplace manlogic

Don't tell them
how bees left
the flowers on their own

and how the flowers went down, too
with nothing but a lucky wind
to spread their kind

Don't let them know
there were rivers
without warnings
and oceans
thick with life
and don't let them know
about coral castles undersea
It would be too cruel.

As we turn photographs to the wall
when a loved one passes
let us burn the images
of all once-living things
as each species disappears
let it be done
lest the children know
what was lost.

Like all good politicians
let us cover our tracks
hide the evidence
of our incalculable avarice
our limitless waste
our misnamed progress
our indifference
lest the children know
our greed.

# Mirror image
*A birthday card*

This is just to say
it took awhile
but I can see you
twenty / twenty now

There you are
hiding in the back row
of my memories
slender willow girl
hair a long pour of redgold
skin translucent
fragile as a Lladro figurine
but blind to it all
focused inward
on bruises
from the night before
how ugly
they made you feel

I see you dance
when no one else knows
sing when you feel sure
no one can hear
I know the words
that explode in your brain
strain to get out
flow through your fingers
make paper music
and I know the why
of your silence

I see you dream of better
than the warzone you called home
a stepfather's rage and lust
a mother too drunk to notice

murdered pets
rundown apartments
everything stripped away
a thrift shop life
see you work after school
to pay for books and fees
you the only grownup
in a house of frightened children

I see you
lead role in the senior play
layers of greasepaint
a heavy-handed mask
to hide behind
acting came naturally
after all, you'd been doing it
all your life
and your siblings
sitting in the front row
in secondhand clothes
playing hooky
from elementary school
so you'd have family there
and I hear you
scold them
walk them back to school

I see it all
even the grit it took
to bear a fatherless child
conceived on prom night
a wild attempt to escape
I hear you sing lullabies
you wish someone
had sung to you

I see you
hiding yourself

hating yourself
oh, how you couldn't stand
the sight of you
how you magnified
freckles into flaws
saw yourself misshapen
wound up anorexic
half dead inside

I see you damaged and brilliant
struggle through two degrees
raise three kids
nurture grandkids
I see you successful
accomplished
yet afraid to live

The mirror still speaks to you
in forked tongues
calls you unworthy

This is to let you know
I can see you now
through eyes
that had to learn
to love you
as you walked
through the center
of hell

This is just to say
it took me sixty-nine years
to see
how strong
how damned
how beautiful
you were.

# Regrets of a sixteenth summer

I don't regret the way the sun dropped low
in summer's sky and brought the twilight on
from liliaceous shades to indigo
the fabled darkness just before the dawn

I don't regret the dawn that never came
nor that the summer ended far too soon
with jasmine giving way to sorrel's flame
as wishing stars fell prey to Hunter's Moon

I don't regret Dame Nature's turning wheel
nor castles made of sand that washed away
I don't regret the love we had to steal
nor any dragons that we had to slay

Yet I am grieved for happiness I lost
and bridges that I burned but never crossed.

# On approaching the age of 69

My birthday comes soon, Mother
and I almost see you there
sitting to the side of me
your velvet dressing gown
wrapped in a fog
of morning-after cigarette smoke
and coffee
shaking your head in disapproval
at "what has become of me
now."

I still mourn you
thirty-eight years later
but you know that
from silent cries
that shake you from eternal sleep
to come and sit awhile
cloaked in disappointment
and dismay.

I look into this mirror
somehow know
you wouldn't have handled
age so very well
you who died
skin smooth
eyes bright
still an interest
in lacy lingerie
still looking
for the prince who never showed.

You couldn't have dealt
with the totality of age
its grandiose demands

bones glass-blown by time
the fragile skin grown thin
scars and wrinkles that mar
tattoo this outer shell
with well-mapped memories.

These days, I almost understand
how you'd lost everything
but beauty
died rather than let it go.

# Poems from
# Season of Mists
# & More

# Hanging tough

Wind gathers the lake in her arms
unleashes in bright ripples
stars that hide beneath
geese honk like old men with sinusitis
they rise into expected V formation
and make their exit
somewhere a swan trumpets
voice belying the grace and glide
it too will go
everything speaks autumn and leaving
all is in order, I think
the die cast
Yet what is this small rebellion
this unexpected hope?

Red and renegade
against a cobalt sky
one tree decidedly deciduous
stubbornly hangs on
among her barren brothers
whose limbs went leafless
with the first strong breeze

While the last maple seeds helicopter down
pirouette in sync with a vertical chorus line
of pin oak, beech and dogwood
this one defies the final dance
eternal as an evergreen

Her leaves refuse the internal push and prod
of gestating buds determined to take their place
she milks this indefinite life
for all it's worth
roots dug in
colors waving proud
as any battle flag

I believe
she will make it through
crimson and daring counterpoint
to April's blush and bloom

I believe
we will see spring.

## Harbinger

Outside my window
eating spring
this early squirrel
tired of winter's stash
climbs gingerly
amongst the long
gestating branches
to find this
unborn
tender-petaled
bud bearing
promises

and tastes the
dim-remembered
something-not-a-winter
and bright within her
something-like-a-mystery
sparks
leaps
hums
in almost
celebration and
it is enough
to be a squirrel
who waits for
something
nameless
that will come
wrapped in flowers
and warm
surprise.

## Surviving April

No ordinary child
April woke
a thing possessed
recalcitrant and strange
she stormed in belligerent
drowned out birdsong
with raucous cries
of starling and crow
skies went grey and glower
as she stomped homicidal
her muddy boots
made of my garden
a cemetery of blossoms
dead and scattered
like some macabre confetti
she strangled seeds in grubby fists
and mangled tender roots

there was no distracting her
with infinite treasure
of butterflies or happy hum of bees

she was death on a rampage
in the garb of a wayward daughter
laying waste to everything
joy and hope
wilted and gone
she has aborted spring
in a tantrum of tornadic winds
a betrayal of darksome floods
till only bare earth
and stark, wet bark
remain

This morning: consolation
with the turn of a calendar's page
the blue-eyed promises of May
wary, I scan the horizon
and seeing only sunlight
hearing the song
of a gun shy Carolina wren
I pick up a tentative spade
seedlings of rosemary, garlic and rue
I venture forth
to do what I must do
begin again.

## Cherries Jubilee

I love how the cherry
blossoms before leaving
how she cannot contain
her pink exuberance
after winter's long sequester
soon petals drift and scatter
like the laughter of small children
soon leaves come
soothing with shade
soon fruit plumps
with juice and joy
but for now
she raises exultant limbs to heaven
bearing tribute
of flowers fantastic
praising
praising.

# Grace in spring

Here to this earth held at gunpoint
hijacked for treasures
stone-fracked
bought and sold
as though paper could hold
or law bind
what belongs to no one

Here to this world
where men sleepwalk oblivious
to April who slumbers
with her doors unlocked
she who everywhere now
lets down her hair
in tangled cascade
of vines and flowers
who carpets the forest
with dark mosses
who breaks open her paintbox
of colors dreamed all winter
and with a single stroke
Monets the wildwood
she whose blue-eyed morning
stretches over all of us

Though machines grind
and politicians rage
though tinny radio commercials
and warhawking moneymongers
drown out birdsong
though manunkind robotic trudges
every ticktock day

Here to this place
once more, a grace unmerited
now comes (inexplicably) spring.

# Time-out

I woke to flowerbeds
beaten by storms
as though some celestial referee
has called time-out
and for a moment
spring's progress is forbidden
she stands naked
her Disney colorations
gone all drab
trees wisteria'd only yesterday
in liliaceous glory
fade to grey
white petals of the dogwood
fragile and fallen, translucent
against rainsoaked bark
clouds glower
making of midday
an otherwhere twilight
diaphanous curtains of soft rain
move through the forest
in shifting shades of silver
birds that sang Vivaldi
are still and songless now
forget their quest for food
shiver on wet branches
heads tucked beneath their wings

there is a stillness in the journey
that takes us to places unintended
there is a silence
deeper than any prayer.

# Flora

Out of the cold tomb of winter
we see the proof again
how bonds of death are broken
by such slender fingers
how it cannot hold her

Crowned in vernal splendor
cloaked in garlands of lilac and pansy
she comes

Made of air and light and wild honey
summoned by the deep ache
of life for itself
she comes

Her breath precious as early violets
in the green leafed morning
she blooms

Again she teaches
the gentle lesson
that life will out
she dances
and makes a lie of sin

Stripped of the dark
we held onto
we wipe the bitter ashes
from our foreheads
awed by her presence
we are aspen in the Pando grove
trembling as one before her

See now
even the sun
is kindled by her glory!

# Invocation to a new spring

Let dawn break in every cell
let the shackles of winter fall away
and the imprisoned go free
in this blue-eyed morning of forever
let the voice of a child answer all questions
let earth turn sunward and warm our frigid souls
let everyone sing in praise of a new Eden
let us erase old stories
that rage of gods we have created
for they have made us
a ravenous murder of crows
and let everything change
let there be no strangers among kindred
let spring come.

## Starting gait

Spring shyly ambles in
across the land
on wobbly legs
too young to gallop
gait uncertain
she falters
and winter so unkindly
rushes back to rein her in
and harness with icy webs
fragile blossoms
but spring is strong
gets her legs quickly
and it's clear
she's the only filly in this race
winter finds himself outpaced
there is no room for him
for now is the hour
of tender throated lilies
and newborn flowers
though storms rage
and bow them low
they rise defiant
true sun glows crepuscular
through cathedral windows
of each soul
so human
and so full of hope.

# March

World sleeps winter
dreams dark
hope sits featherless
in the bonecage
song frozen in its throat
easy to abandon
such a thing
our primal selves
retrace the long way
back to the cave
where we feared
as infants
that Mother
who has merely stepped
into another room
will not return

Outside
wind shifts
sun slants
world tilts
wheel turns
here find no blight
this is the harvest of light
fruit of solstice longing
on this naked skull of a world
this is the borning

Gaia swings her daughter upside down
and she is a child again
cheeks dawn-flushed
in the bluesky morning
she giggles butterflies
a joyous scatter
of ladybugs and peepers

bobwhites and bluebirds
flit, leap, fly and flutterby
from her chubby fingers
life tickles everywhere
she laughs unstoppable
till blossoms tumble from her pockets
like pennies
to purchase our redemption.

## Storm song

It's not yet dawn, and thunder shakes my bed,
forbidding weather, funnel clouds descend
just to the north and all across the zone
in which I live, while even more impend.

Azaleas droop, their brilliant colors gone,
the winds have flattened older, stronger stems,
confetti'd petals decorate the lawn,
across the way, the cherry's lost its limbs.

A sudden intermission – all is still,
except for patter of the rain outside,
when unexpectedly, I hear the song
of one brave bird that will not be denied.

When storms and darkness overtake the spring,
oh, let me be the bird who dares to sing.

# Eviction of Orion

Oh, blind Orion leave these heavens now
your form, your dog, your bloody hunter's kill
for we have tolerated you too long
the struggle decimates both heart and will

Let blossoms purge our memory of you
let crocus, daffodil and meadowbright
let milkweed, poppies, graceful curl of fern
replace your frigid tyranny and blight

Come home now birds, on shining pinions wing
come butterfly and bee to pollenate
each blossom, while earth wears her Easter dress
Persephone's return we celebrate

Thus go away, grave hunter, from this sky!
the wheel has turned; now let cruel winter die.

# The price of spring

Winter bullied its way
into this wildwood
buried each acre
beneath a foot of snow
the birds flew long ago
left branches silent
as the grave
yet orphaned beauty sleeps
a threadbare thing
secluded in these woods
and silent dreams
in knotted limbs
gestating spring
when gardeners strip
the burlap shrouds away
and crocuses emerge
when swift and robin
return to nest
and the face of earth
disturbs her rest
to look full upon the sun
and wait the plow
she pays no mind
to iron-clawed furrow
nor the harrow soon to come
for this is spring
and well she knows
there is a price to everything.

# Homecoming

The air is a-buzz with wings
bird to butterfly
bee to dragonfly
flit, fly and flutter by

cherry trees lifting petticoats to heaven
full-blossomed defiance
caught mid-cartwheel
kicking up chaos
in can-can regalia
long-limbed show-offs
in ruffles and bloomers
late and early
daffodils and Japanese magnolia
crocus and iris and tulips cover places
old winter (that cold-handed lover)
has relinquished at last
bright spindled forsythia
lilies and redbud
double flowering peach
too much is not enough

this is earth in her party dress

and all because Persephone
called ahead to say
*Mama – I'm comin' home!*

# Rites of spring

here to this place of unity, we come in spirit
fragrant of greening earth and bearing early flowers
we come

people from Kenya with painted faces
shy as fawns, they bloom quiet from the long shadows of Eden

in China, a pearl farmer leaves incubating moons
to meditate in cherry blossoms

and somewhere in the Mediterranean
a tired old fisherman suddenly turns his boat home
remembering the brown ankles of his wife

here at home, a farmer leaves furrowed soil
and barefoot children dance, their eyes like bright gems
laughing in the new light

old women don ruffles, forget their places
remember forbidden kisses and evenings redolent of lilac

old men leave chess games in the park
dream of singing doo-wop on street corners
pack of Luckies rolled up in t-shirt sleeves and hard
muscled arms bronzed, suddenly young again

lawyers lay briefcases aside
senators forget why they were making rules
soldiers forget why they were fighting
remember poppy fields and picnics

preachers find empty pews
rush to see what all the commotion is about
discover a better pulpit

no one is blind to this bluesky morning
no one is deaf to this rhythm

earth shakes the pebbles from her shoes
forgets for a springtime moment
the bruises that we make.

## Spring, anyhow

These limbs are laden with blossoms
but do not break
they obliterate the sky with pink tenacity
though acid rain falls
and petals cling pallid and frail
to the black bark
nothing breaks this roseate morning
though the petals are leaden
and their weight has become everything
for losing even one
is immediately noticeable
and leaves a hollow place of echoed prayers
and remembered flutings of birds
nothing breaks here
but bends and sways in hurricane winds
man-blighted roots hold firm
though the sad earth
quakes and trembles
and at night the moon
caught in this net of branches
holds the sea still
her eyes remembering
what swam beneath
what flew above

For it is spring, anyhow
in this place we are destroying
it is spring, anyhow
that tries to dance arthritic
through these limbs
where nothing seems too heavy to bear
nor no burden so oppressive
as gardens lost
as these blessings
fragile and forgotten.

# Invocation

Lady of secrets,
come forth!
Careless girl,
bearing the marks of
your dark addiction
like a badge –
licking your fingers,
mouth bloomed garnet
with the forbidden juice.

Come, shameless beauty,
trailing your bat-winged babies behind you!

Dance down the woodland,
laughing in your tattered gown,
feigning innocence once more!
We – the guilty – will believe you.

Consume us entirely,
Lady of burning flowers!
Drape us with green and with garland.

Sweet, demented child –
lover of excess,
make us suffer
your eccentricities again.
Give us over once more
to this tyranny of Spring.

How we crave
the honey and the madness!

Come, Persephone!
Make your Mama smile!

## Warning

Don't get sidetracked by spring
whatever you do
don't look at that apple tree
flaunting her blossoms in the wind
shameless and out of control
shifting lace
abuzz and aflutter
coyly revealing limbs
anxious for fruit
*type . . . anything*

*google obscure subjects*
*t3X7 y0uR fri3nd5 In L337 spe@K*

whatever you do
don't enter that Garden
don't give yourself over to Beauty
she'll knock you to your knees
and there you'll be
sprawled on the path
with a goofy look on your face
like Paul on the road to Damascus
for the veil has been rent
and you've glimpsed
the Holy of Holies
and now you just aren't
with the program

people gather around you
dial 911
take photos with their cell phones
post your pathetic self on YouTube
facebook their friends
*OMG OMG OMG*
offer you bottled water
and a religious tract

while somewhere
hovering above your own body
you see
the Light within the light
and drink
the never bottled
pure unenhanced
completely unmessed with
living water
from the original well-
spring.

# Come, she will

April comes at last
after spring's false starts and stalls
swallows have returned
soon their wide-mouthed babies
occupy the old barn's rafters
window boxes bloom pink and red
butterfly bush entices
swallowtail and hummingbird
sunlight smoothes away
rough edges of the ragged soul
life regenerates
each feather of the starving spirit
and it soars in jubilation

The old man knows
how fragile as crystal glass
each numbered April is
at noon
he props his rake
against the shed
sits for lunch
with his wife of fifty years
who twists an errant curl
and coyly smiles
he winks
they laugh like children
speak of things that lie forgotten
when snow is deep
but this afternoon
memories spring up like poppies
it's lemonade and cakes on the veranda
a conversation of eyes and hands
as Hoagy Carmichael sings
through scratch and crackle
of an ancient LP

viburnum scents the air
till day declines
peepers sing their sleepy hymns
fireflies swing early lanterns
eternal stars appear
and evening falls.

# Respite

Deep in the sugar-blossomed orchard
spring catches in the throat of each bloom
pink with nectar promises

heavy with buzz of bees
dreaming honey-laden fruit to come
this ancient cherry tree
beckons with shade
a dusty wanderer
who turns from roadside Jiffy Mart
leaves billboard clutter
and afternoon sales calls behind
climbs the paint-peeled fence
that separates this holy of holies
from hum and drum of market-
driven life

to lie beneath the timeless flutter
of branch and bower and bee
to relish vague, familiar longings
for childhood's stolen cherry-
pleasured afternoons.

# Wildflowers

Blessed be the mongrel weed
proud beside the pedigreed blossoms
in my garden now – bastard blooms
still somehow rained upon
and sunned the same
as those that have a legal name.

Errant seeds that somersault
upon a feckless summer breeze
find good earth and soundless root
as loved by bees as fancy kin
in windowboxes on the Cape.

They're flowers – just misunderstood
by those demanding heritage
their trumpet throats, their open mouths
seducing hummers, butterflies
alluring as the jasmine vine
pure as lotus and brave as sun
attached to nothing, bound to none.

## Hummingbirds

How in the dapple shadowed early morning,
I fed you summerlong,
applauded every acrobatic flight,
held close each tender trust,
an unsuspecting Eve.

Darwin on Galápagos
would have guessed your family tree,
would have seen what I did not till now.

Disturbing, this resemblance,
feather to scale, needle beak to fang –

how aeons changed you not entirely,
made miniscule your form
and full of grace your aerial ballet,
how jeweled your glistering wings
ignite in early autumn's embered light,
disguise not quite the legacy of iridescent scale –
how ineffable whirr of hovering wings
cannot masque the doomed Edenic hiss.

We all have relatives we'd just as soon forget;
if you forgive my distant kin's neanderthalic ways –
Himmlers, Oppenheimers, and the rest –
I must forgive the serpentine in you.

I shall politely keep our small charade,
pretend I do not know your heritage,
and come next spring, shall fill this font again
with nectar-sweet delight –
fit only for the likes of God and you.

## Late

August is dancing her poppy red-
hot pants off
kicking up her heels out there
to a deafening hum of June bugs
yes-siree-bob, she's raising hell
on the gritty streets of summer
glorifying what is sweaty
and human
noise everywhere
seeps through windows
stealths its way
under doors
thieves concentration
and now some devil
turns on the corner fire hydrant
miniature heathens
loosed from studies and useful chores
frolic in prismed spray
squealing their discordant song
of rapture

when all I want is late
October, red about the maples
and predictable
as syrup on pancakes
wind out of a marine blue sky
that bears a chill
indifferent as marble
a good pot of tea
taken in solitude
contemplation
while the world goes

all mists and melancholy
soft violins taking the lead
as notes wend through evergreen
like incense rising
and the wheel of the year
turns toward winter.

# Mabon

Breath of her breath
incense rising
from leafy forest floor
smoke permeates crisp air
fists beat skin drums
we pour libations
of water and sweet wine
adorn her altar
with fruit and grain
celebrate this holy season
as summer heat dies away
by chant and dance
we invoke and bless her
thank her for her bounty
praise her for her beauty
burning now in every tree

Goddess harvest clad
in golds and ambers
earth sleep comes soon
with its silent longing for snow
black limbs silhouette
against grey sky
all is chiaroscuro for a time
earth dreams spring
nothing is shallow
all is hallowed
hollow hammer of flickers
in the distance.

# Evensong

*for Brenda Levy Tate*

Cicada song hovers
over the river
undulates
dragonflies ride
its hum and thrum
to autumnal oblivion
mists rise
failing light slants
hallows burnished leaves
rustle of reeds
gone brown and gold
splash of late fin or feather
welcomes the year's blue hour
as life settles down
to hearthside voices
baskets bear orchard harvests
stubble fields rest easy now
having yielded up
a winter's worth
of food put by
with loving hands
root cellars filled
the cider press groans
and logs split and waiting
by the door
beckon the evening of the year
when everything becomes
a hymn.

# Autumn in the city

Someone opened the ancient codex
chanted the sacred words
and autumn with her small soft rains
slipped in last night
over concrete mountains
between steel spires
vines trailing up old buildings
suddenly flamed out in glory
fire and wine seeped into leaves
as molten light slanted
through dark urban valleys
revealing city trees
no one had even noticed
the stench of dumpsters and hot dog stands
gave way to childhood memories
of bonfires and marshmallows roasting
and magic long forgotten
touched and stirred and wakened

Cell phones fell silent
as passersby sent calls to voicemail
because something else was speaking
the accountant with his bagel and schmear
looked through the coffee shop window
saw something that stopped his pencil mid-equation
leaving him out of balance
and happily confused
weakened by wonder
bullies taunting a girl on the corner
forgot the names they intended to call her
the old men playing checkers
on the courthouse lawn
heard the skitter of leaves
looked up at kaleidoscopic trees
and forgot who was kinged

And for the briefest moment
everyone remembered
what is important.

# Journal entry 10/29/14

Patter of small rain feet
danced a jig beneath my window
woke me up
I took my morning tea out to the porch
where scattered drops clung
to blade and leaf
compelling meditation
and now these old bones ache
from sitting in the mist
and counting things I know
that number considerably diminished
compared to what it was in youth

I know how to wait
right now, it's late October
still no red and yellow incandescence
ignites these trees with shades of autumn
I can wait
for a good north wind
to shake some sense into things
fling color that flames out on every limb
because I know
these maples will stand
lonely and naked soon enough

I know this world was not banged out
nor was it materialized
by some greybeard in the sky
I know it was born
just brush away the grass
and move the stones
you'll see its very belly button
this place was mothered
like a treasured child

that's what birds sing about
if you listen to the lyrics
and I know
what failed babysitters we are

I know better than to look
into a mirror too closely

I know that burdens are more heavy
when carried in the heart
than on the shoulders
I know that forgiven
rarely means forgotten

I know that my tea grows cold
and too soon I must go
where knowing floats on air
like ash
like angels.

## Consecration

Swallows rise
bloom into grey skies
then scatter
above a world lit
by autumn lanterns that dangle
through tangles of scarlet vines
and blackened branches

and from my vantage point
this rock at Morgan's Steep
its face a sculpture roughhewn
wind and water worn
I lay down my sketchbook
humbled by what
charcoal cannot replicate

instead I scan the palette below
Cumberland Plateau
unfurled in patchwork splendor
resembling a quilt
my grandmother might have stitched
to comfort me

in fact, I find myself inclined
within my rebel pagan mind
to believe that she did
and that she watches
from her home in afterwhere
knowing how I love it here
which was to her a sin
but freed from bone and skin
perhaps she understands
and loves me still

and when I squint
autumn Van Goghs the canvas

insane with sorrel
mad with goldenrod
crazed by haystacks and fields
mown or harvested
all kindled by November's
final flames

this conflagration of the old year
consecrates all to evening
with her cold and starry night
she calls us home
to human warmth
before the fire
to the hallowed presence
of each other.

# Plea to Autumn

Burn me, Autumn!

Blind me with your glory
for what is left to see
when you are gone

Dazzle my last vision
with your incandescence
russet red and golden

See how your presence
trembles through these limbs
with your slightest breath
how color scintillates

Incinerate me
on a pyre
fire fragranced
by your leaves
piled high in every lane

Scatter my ashes
on the brisk wings
of your waking winds

Lay me gently
across the lap of April
to feed new life
that I, too, may shine
among your branches
upon your bright return.

# October Song

The wind goes picking apples, and they fall
she doesn't care to choose by cultivar
the Granny Smith, Delicious, Delrouval
all find their way to press or canning jar

The wind goes picking apples, and they fall
regardless of estate or pedigree
befreckled, bruised, gourmet, she gathers all
and none escapes her reaping that I see

Forget her sweet, flirtatious dance in May
through heavy-honeyed blossoms on each limb
her whispered breezes that began the play
grow colder with her final harvest hymn

We line her greedy baskets, one and all
the wind goes picking apples, and we fall.

## Thanksgiving

Before we descend into winter
purple twilights, numbing glare of snow
and ice, let us delight in November gold
embrace its small rains, dying leaves
wet and bright against black bark
its mists that shawl the mountains

let us mark remnants
of Monarchs that dare
the stark and final nectared hour
and farewell cries of geese
in V-formation silhouette
against the grey and glower

let us hold these days wholly
this season of cider and smoke
and know that nothing is final

yet, let us praise feasts
prepared by hands diligent and loving
crops gathered in
by hands rough and torn
firewood stacked and waiting

and while in every corseted garden
tasteful and blueprinted
April slumbers
oh, let us honor the wild, wild fields
where rampant runs the sorrel's flame
punctuated by late marigolds
and weeds that do not even have a name.

# On defying the natural order

*In loving disagreement with Radcliffe Squires, Robert Frost and Gerard Manley Hopkins*

If the light
in autumn's final leaf
did not fall
or fade
or sink
to grief
but danced
into winter
a solitary wonder

refused to grace
the forest floor
leafmeal there
and nothing more
unwithered
daring everything
the deadly frost
the shock of cold
could shake the blight
and still burn gold
without a flicker

if that light
held strong and knew
another spring
its sap renewed
in every vein
and summer, too

o, for such hope
in such a light

that never dimmed
but dared the night
rebuked for all
the killing child
whose arrogance
would have it fall
and take its place

o, such a light
so dark an art
could topple
Eden's applecart.

# Windfall meditation

Windfall mercy
unburdened boughs
lit by splintered shafts of golden light
sweet, this holy circle gathered round
for the likes of deer and me

here on my knees
midst freckled blessings
free for the taking
I find more answers
to the prayers I make
than any imagined voice
in domed cathedral could convey

I've stitched my life's meandering design
heedless of any pattern made
pricked my fingers
stained with my own blood
this haphazard creation
patchworked with whatever colored thread
I found at hand

no harp-filled heaven waiting overhead
no serpent lurking in amongst the fruit
no hell below except by my devise
each prayer ascended
plummets back to me
to answer or withhold

the deer within this fragrant circle
sees only fruit, questions not
the wind that shook the bough
seeks no serpent nor any god
and so it seems with me

regardless of the days I praised him
from whom all blessings flowed
I found him missing
just when needed most
and now I walk this autumn path alone
knowledge like a knife within my core
nothing is borrowed here
and nothing owed
there is no question
every rib is mine

the doe leaps graceful
through the shadowed wood
hears not the gun cocked
dies still tasting
the serendipitous feast

I'll move on before I hear her fall
apples a dead weight in my pockets
I'll cross the river before sunset
if no storm has washed away the bridge
if no bullet finds me.

# Windfall

Behind
the hundred orchard rows
where lithe-limbed trees
in sprayed and pruned perfection
lift tame treasures
through mellow Indian Summer
till fruit is finished
grown unblemished
red and round
more suited for a photograph
than eating

Past
tall grasses
long ignored
spared by mowers
where crickets harmonize
at evening's edge
where owl calls low
as fireflies dim their lanterns
with the year's decline

There
a vestige of the elder farm remains
preceding advent of machine
relic of the days
when human hands took
autumn fruit as free
as any Adam

Lone surviving tree
gnarled and ancient
Sequestered deep within

concentric rings
does something like a memory lie?
Tire swings that creaked
and spanned a score of summer lives
suffering freckled Robin Hoods
to pilfer her green fruit
and climb her patient ladders
into manhood
while shaded soft
beneath her latticed boughs
beguiled by flutter
butterfly and blossom
drowsy maidens slumbered
dreaming royals
sure to come

Her ragged leaves stir
just slightly tinged with russet
arthritic limbs
twisted and determined
to hold with firm resolve
her happy burden
irregular and speckled
ruby globes
grown pendulous and plumped
and heavy honeyed
waiting wayward child
or hungry vagrant
to climb and claim
her treasured harvest
autumnal and sweet

Then comes a storm too bitter
unexpected
and windfall apples cast a holy circle
of premature bounty

Let us take
this tempting orb
before it spoils
cut cross-
wise mark the story
secreted within seeds
in poignant pattern
knowledge half-forgotten
behold the perfect pentacle
the core within the fruit
air, fire, water, earth and Spirit
eternal equilibrium
the partnership
of nature and divine
before the fall
before machine
when human hands took
autumn fruit as free
as any Adam.

*Kore's sacred fruit is the apple. When an apple is cut through its equator, both halves will reveal a pentagram shape at the core, with each point on the star containing a seed. Each point symbolic, respectively, of the elements of nature and Spirit, the sum symbolizing balance and perfection. The Roma (Gypsies) call this core the Star of Knowledge.*

# Appalachian autumn

Below, the land grew sweet with goldenrod,
while through the rising mists
shone incandescent these leaves,
into which a molten glory poured,
made sacred the most common weed.

Sorrel flamed with pokeberries burning blue,
each a new Grail,
each bearing strange communion,
hot and holy,
into the dying light
that wheeled in a mid-December sky,
turned cold as stone toward winter.

And spiraled incense
from each chimney on the ridge
hallowed, held close each moment,
before it fell away to graceful night.

So deep the silence here,
it had a song.
So still the silence here,
water running underground
could play its hollow notes against the wind.

Spring cannot hold this chalice
in her tender hands –
here, all are tread into a vintage
rare and holy,
this late and deep awareness
of life as it closes:
this gold of burning out in grace.

Yet each branch holds birth like treasure,
each leaf pushed from its place
by new life anxious for April,

and blanketed beneath
all that have fallen
sleeps Spring, fertile and waiting.

## Gathered in

Now autumn with her meditative sigh
sweeps cool across the fields of harvest grain
the cider press awaits, the pumpkins lie
abundant, blest by fertile earth and rain

with summer's heated passion finally spent
the logs are stacked anticipating snow
while leaves abandon limbs in bright descent
all burnished with an incandescent glow

the world's at rest, the year is winding down
as nature burns the residue away
and smoky incense hallows farm and town
while cricket vespers rise at close of day

a book, a purring cat, a pot of tea
oh, tell me, April, what are you to me?

# Into this Eden

Let me not go down
into the earth that bore me
let not flesh sink
to alabaster bone
in silence
darkness
and alone

> *Once within the Everglades*
> *dazzled by gilded reeds*
> *and dappled shade*
> *beneath a bright*
> *and cerulean sky*
> *I watched*
> *color and light*
> *conspire as friends*
> *to shift and part*
> *and suddenly reveal*
> *a golden panther*
> *in the splinter of a moment's end*
> *then saw it just as quickly fade*
> *to camouflage again*

Let me go down so
myself disperse
meld into autumn light
merge and mingle
with shadows cast
by birds and dragonflies
let my words rise
a faint incense
upon the breeze
an almost-heard inflection
that sings hollow
rings of hope
within the sound

of water running softly underground
o let the meter that was mine
the living rhyme
that pumped my heart
and gave me life
and any worthy dream
I might have had
be one
with every glory burning bright
upon this earth

not high above
nor in between
nor yet below
but into this Eden
let me go
thus let me stay.

# No Hunting

*for Ted*

Papa and you are the only two men I ever knew
who understood
that being human is about feeding things
and now you put up signs
around that church you built
in the forest
to tell hunters
whatever goes on tender hooves
between the trillium and the ladyslippers
gone down for winter
has found itself already
was never lost and
so they may not come
to hunt it
with their right to bear arms
they never open
to spill its blood
and spoil this earth
that what is found here
has no season

And when hunters come
arguing that the poor bastards
will overbreed and starve
will you feed them
like you feed the birds
and the rest of us?

These are men who look into
soft-eyed life
and drop it to earth

with a sound so sharp and
so accustomed
they don't even blink anymore

Put up your signs
if bullets read
maybe what goes here can
walk safely
put up your barbed wire
so fox and deer
can sleep safe
and dream free

You came here for a freedom
you could not reach
you came here
and put a stained glass window
in a temple to the wilderness
because you lost something
and you found something

Now fence your freedom in
unroll the barbed wire
post your sanctuary
but watch your back
and wear bright colours
sleep with one eye open
and put a sign up in the temple
to remind yourself:

*Between what is found and what is lost*
*between what is safe and what is free*
*walk the hunted.*

# Thank you note
*The agnostic's Thanksgiving*

I want to thank whoever
is responsible for
these leaves whose centers
are igniting now with some
internal sunset
incandescent luminescent
embered red and amber
ending that is not

*I want to thank someone*

I want to thank whoever
is responsible for
the molten gold spreading
through tops of
birches catching
like wildfire leaping
limb to limb
and the ruby-feathered cardinal
who just lit
perfectly
in those branches

*I want to thank someone*

I want to thank whoever
is responsible for
these foreign birds
that felt winter in their bones
and found shelter here
and also for
migrating Monarchs

hanging upside-down
bright-winged additions
to trees already radiant

*I want to thank someone*

I want to thank whoever
is responsible for
that Joseph's coat
tossed casually
across the valley
that patchwork
of honey and loden
harvested or fallow
or going down to stubble
and for pokeberries
good for nothing but
purple luminosity
and for ornamental gourds
and all such
useless things
whose only excuse
is beauty

*I have to thank someone*

I want to thank whoever
is responsible for
this glorious battered world
that still struggles to her feet
regardless of our blows
and turns a graceful pirouette
toward winter
still does this breathtaking
tango with a dying sun

without fanfare
or applause
or even our approval

*I just need to thank someone for the dance.*

# For a swinger of birches

*for Robert Frost*

We swung on birches, you and I.
You took me down to the pasture, too,
and taught me well along the way
to question what a wall should do.

You led me down the left-fork road.
I found it rocky, bare and steep,
for I was soft with city ways,
but you had promises to keep.

You showed me how to clear that spring,
and how to know which road to take.
You versed me well in country things,
the difference a choice can make.

You were acquainted with the night –
a child, I didn't understand.
Your poems began in sweet delight;
in age, their wisdom takes my hand.

You told me nothing gold can stay.
Your legacy gives that the lie.
Your lover's quarrel is in time out;
we'll get back to it bye-and-bye.

## Dark lullaby

Just lately
this persistent rise and fall
of nonexistent cicada chorus
ringing in my ears
recalls how childhood evenings fell

how the sun abruptly dropped
below Old Farm Hill's crest
an exhausted orange ball
so done with day
how liliaceous morning skies

turned uncontrollably indigo
and like some small Neanderthal
I feared the sun would not return

how I put away playthings
and reluctant took
the once bright path
that downhill now
turned ominous and dark
deep with gathered shadows
mysterious with owls
and flap of wings invisible
heavy with howl
of Papa's old hunting dog
and fearsome hidden things

how with silver-fingered moon
insistent on my shoulders
I unwilling left
always wanting more
and feared the night and nothingness
of sleep

then once I cleared the crest
and started down
how the many-candled window
of Mama's house
grew bright against the dark
how fireflies lifted
tiny, ineffective lanterns
toward the stars
as ebb and rise of cicada
sang me home.

## Grace

When birds feel winter stirring in their bones,
they come to me for seed and suet and grain,
bits of berries, fruit, peanut butter
pressed in pine cones hung with bright ribbon.

Too cold to sit out on my porch,
it becomes an avian restaurant,
dishes hanging, seeds scattered,
things filter down,
chickadees and finches on the feeders,
cardinals and jays upon the floor.

I'll clean it up come spring,
but not before I've left enough
string and feathers, yarn and twigs
to help with April nesting.

Why this brings me joy, I cannot say.
I do not watch them, draw my blinds,
and let them live in peace,
in some small comfort without fear.

I never made up ten restricting rules, with corollaries
and threats of eternal roasting on a spit,
if they fail to straighten up and fly right.

Nor do I peek into their nests
to ascertain if one has strayed
and found another's mate more pleasing.

Nor do I ask for a tenth
of whatever wage a sparrow earns,
or require that I be honored
on certain days of the week.

Nor do I demand confessions
and weigh their happy wings with heavy hearts,
nor yet prefer a redbird to a blue.

I do not know when one has fallen
prey to prowling cats, or when a boy steals
bright blue eggs to show at school,
(though I would stop him if I could).

Wren to oriole, they go their way unfettered,
and I go mine without a thought,
except that I fed something
beautiful.

# Exit

This recalcitrant winter
roars its loudmouth winds
yet must backtrack
grumble and grouse in defeat
till there's just enough breeze
to mount a kite upon
or help a gossamer parachute
deliver a dandelion
to some unwary gardener's lawn

For even in this purple dusk
spring casts her handful of stars
across the sky
and sets earth's destiny
the ancient wheel turns
the snowcrust breaks
to bear the daffodil
which stands at dawn
and with a rebel cry shouts
*I am alive*
and I for one am glad
to see the old intruder go
dragging his great bag
overstuffed with sorrows
he is akin to death
and far as I know
he is no cousin of mine

A bastard child, I was born
of autumn and the spring
those seasons of extreme
that fall between
bear no relation
and are at best
tedious and most unwelcome guests.

# The Visitor

Ah, sweet, bedraggled April,
purveyor of annual infection,
scattering your pollen on my doorstep.
Who beckoned you here
with your drifts of cherry blossoms,
your blue-eyed boys pushing lawnmowers
and aphrodisiacs?

Who summoned you
fresh from the netherworld,
costumed in Goodwill
tatters, knock-knee'd, biting
one fingernail and twisting
a curl, stirring the pot
of rancid promises and battered dreams?

I know your wanton ways, sister,
your languid eyes, deceptive sighs,
wilted narcissus in your hair
a poor attempt to hide the tangles
buried there.

What fooled me at 17 isn't likely to at 60.

*Got a poisoned apple in your basket?*
*An asp hiding in the nosegay?*
*A bite worse than the bark*
*of that dog in heat up the street?*

I'll not invite you in.
As the crucifix above my door implies,
werewolves, vampires, April and the like
are not welcome here.
Peddle your wares to someone else,
someone who cares, while I care less,
someone without a memory.

# Praisepoem

Praise to You by many names called,
by none defined,
Praise to You who will not be contained,
You of the limitless where
and the boundless here,
For You have filled my blood with words this day,
and play your happy songs upon my bones like a flute.
Glory be to You for the exuberance of life,
for this dance that does not cease.
Let me see You in all things created:

Glory to You for the gaudiness of flowers,
for outrageous roses never told
that pink and coral and scarlet are not properly worn together,
for flamevine in passionate abundance
dancing in the blue and golden morning,
Glory to You for this ignorance of flowers,
for they have not been informed
that beauty commands a price,
but display their splendor
to the poorest among us who walk the field with open eyes.

Glory to You for the wonder of night sky,
for the glittering extravagance of so many stars.
Glory to You for the miracle of morning,
shattering darkness into fragments that scatter
butterflies in glad profusion across the blossoming dawn sky.

Glory to You for this cacophony of birdsong,
For melodies of skylark and disharmonies of crow,

For plagiarizing mockingbird
and ineffable whisper of hummingbird wings.
Glory to You for all feathered flight
and also for the common caterpillar, who waking
from long sleep finds wings bejeweled
like a gift from morning:
What excess of joy bears him up,
with blossoms as his only fit companions.

Praise to You for marshland that stretches in oceanic waves
of brown and golden reeds against the sky,
How filled with Life is the tiniest drop of its water.
Glory to You for the ruby-throated lizard
and the darkness of swamp that sings with
toad and serpent and cry of heron,
with vulture and with snowy ibis,

each with a place and a beauty
that You have ordained.

Glory to You for brown and russet, for gray and indigo,
for the thousand-colored shadows
of this deepstill meditation of reed and bog,
for the treasure of reflection:
Where water stands, I find pieces of sky.

Glory to You for saltwater, fresh water,
amniotic waters of the womb of Life,
For our blood that contains the same chemistry,
documenting our heritage, our source, our family.
Glory to You for the shattering of birth,
Glory to You for the wisdom of the pain of giving life,
for it reminds us that we enter this consciousness
both heirs and indebted.

Glory to You for the magnificence of stone,
for its strong and silent singing, as it teaches us
the virtue of simply being.
Glory to You for the verdant grandeur of forest,
for the bountiful home of deer and dove,
of rabbit and fox,
for whom You provide unquestioned.

I sit upon the earth and feel Your pulse beneath me.
I sit in the limbs of trees and know I rest in Your arms
like a sleepy child.
I look to the infinite reaches of space, and You are there,
laughing down at me!
I look through a microscope into a molecule of matter, and behold:
You are there, laughing up at me!

Glory to You for all limitless things:
for sand, for stars, for the subatomic world,
For through them, we see You most truly;
In them, we see You most clearly.

Oh, Inexhaustible:
You who have no limitations,
You who scoff at boundaries,
Oh, Everlasting:
You who are,
You who have been,
You who shall be ever,

Oh, Unutterable:
Your creations in all their wonder
are but pale shadows of Your Most Holy Self
How beyond imagination,
the infinite beauty of Your Face.

# About the poet

Carla Martin-Wood has been a widely published poet since 1978. Recently retired from her career in the rat race world of advertising, she is relishing her newfound freedom and happily embraces her station as the Witch on Yellowhammer Hill.

The author of seven full-length books of poetry prior to *The Witch on Yellowhammer Hill*, Carla's most recent collection was *Eiswein* (The Pink Petticoat Press, 2015). She has also authored eight chapbooks, most recently *Season of Mists* (The 99% Press, 2012).

A copy of Carla's chapbook, *Garden of Regret* (Pudding House Publications Chapbook Series, 2009), resides in the Special Collections & University Archives at Stanford University, contributed by the renowned Russian poet, essayist and dramatist, Yevgeny Yevtushenko.

Carla's poems have appeared in a plethora of journals and numerous anthologies in the US, England, and Ireland since 1978. With a background of 13 years in theatre, she has performed her work from the hallowed University of The South at Sewanee to legendary Greenwich Village.

She has been nominated for The Pushcart Prize more than a dozen times, for Best of the Net twice, and is listed in Poets & Writers.

Carla has been a lifelong political and social activist. Her introduction to activism was as one of four white teens who fought their way through picket lines to break the white boycott of a high school in Birmingham, Alabama during the violent racial conflicts of 1963. She continued as an activist for human rights, the anti-war movement and NOW through the 1980s. Her current interests lie in preservation of the earth, universal healthcare and gun control.

# Acknowledgements

# Photography & Art

# Publications

This book includes over 50 new or previously unpublished poems. The other poems have previously appeared, as follows:

Most of the chapbook *Season of Mists* (The 99% Press, 2012) appears as part of the second section of the book.

From the chapbook, *Songs from the Web* (Bitter Wine Press, 1986): *womanpoem*

From *Garden of Regret* (Pudding House Chapbook Series: 2008), *Bitch* and *Bliss*

From *Flight Risk* (Fortunate Childe Publications, 2009): *Cherry-on-Top; Grace; Make me a Nine; Flight Risk*

From the chapbook, *Absinthe & Valentines* (Flutter Press, 2011): *The Last Magick* and *The Visitor*

From *Into the Windfall Light* (The Pink Petticoat Press, 2011): *Hummingbirds; Rites of spring; For a swinger of birches; Respite*

From *Stories from Eden* (The Pink Petticoat Press, 2012): *Medusa; Circe; Lilith; Magdalen; Trial; Are you scared yet?; Way of the Raven; Don't tell Mama; Don't tell the children; Spring, anyhow*

From *How we are loved* (Fortunate Childe Publications, 2012): *Praisepoem*

From *out of the bonecage singing* (The Pink Petticoat Press, 2014): *Consecration; Mabon; Exit*

From *Eiswein* (The Pink Petticoat Press, 2015): *The beautiful dead; The one; Autumn in the city; Winter apocalypse; Hanging tough; Come, she will; Homecoming; On defying the natural order; Snowblind*

*Thanksgiving, Dark Lullaby, Auld Lang Syne, Crone's Counsel,* and *In which I am An Cailleach Bhéara,* The Linnet's Wings, Ireland (2015 – 2016).

# Also by this author

Eiswein
*The Pink Petticoat Press*

Stories from Eden
*The Pink Petticoat Press*

How we are loved
*Fortunate Childe Publications*

Into the Windfall Light
*The Pink Petticoat Press*

Flight Risk & Other Poems
*Fortunate Childe Publications*

One flew east
*Fortunate Childe Publications*

Songs from the Web (encore)
*Fortunate Childe Publications*

Absinthe & Valentines
*Flutter Press*

The Last Magick
*Fortunate Childe Publications*

HerStory
*Fortunate Childe Publications*

Feed Sack Majesty
*Fortunate Childe Publications*

Redheaded Stepchild
*Pudding House Chapbook Series*

Garden of Regret
*Pudding House Chapbook Series*

www.ingramcontent.com/pod-product-compliance
Lightning Source LLC
Chambersburg PA
CBHW072003040426
42447CB00009B/1460